AF413242

OUTSIDE THE DARK

Photography and words by Chris Van Kirk

Dedication

In memory of my beautiful mother.

I will miss you forever.

Your son,
Chris

If we don't see the future,
in the present, we are blind...

I WALK WALK

We bow to lazy idleness,
And, no doubt, the doubting Mind.

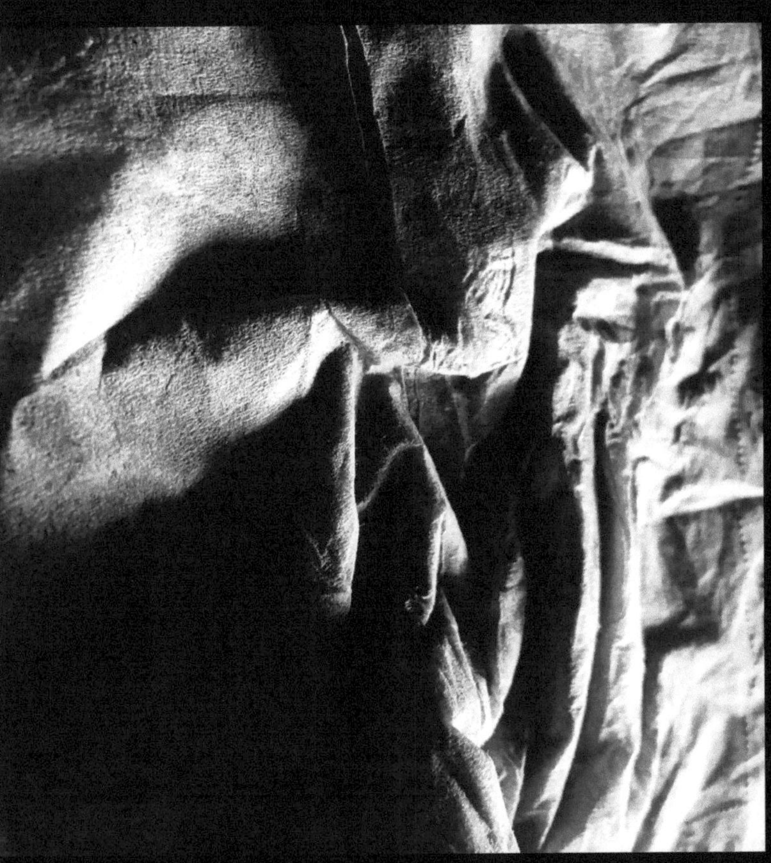

In bed, in sleep, in Night's dreamland
pesters the unforgiving Night,

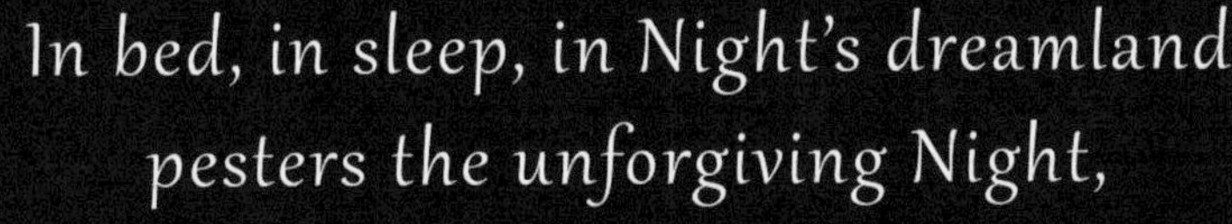

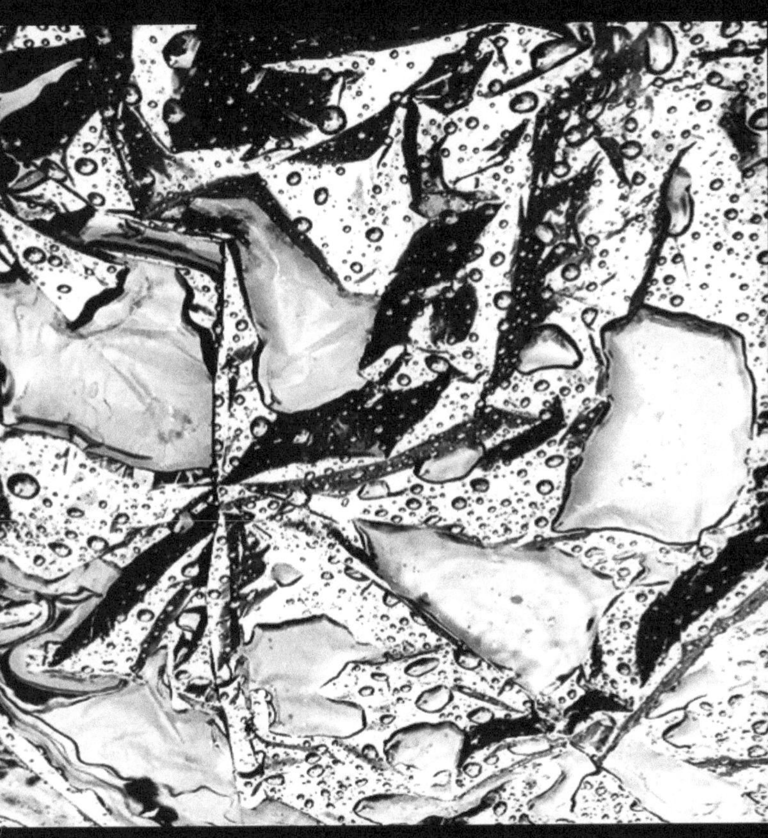

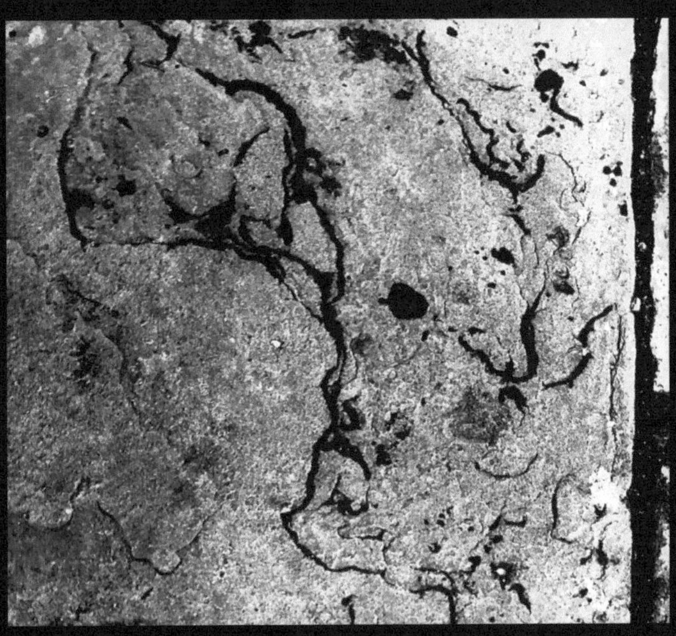

My Mind's eye sees,
as through a mirror;

What's left has now become right.

Metronome sings it's tuneless song,
synced flawlessly, my beating heart.

Mundaneness reigns; day in, day out.
Sweet Hope's taste, now, is tart.

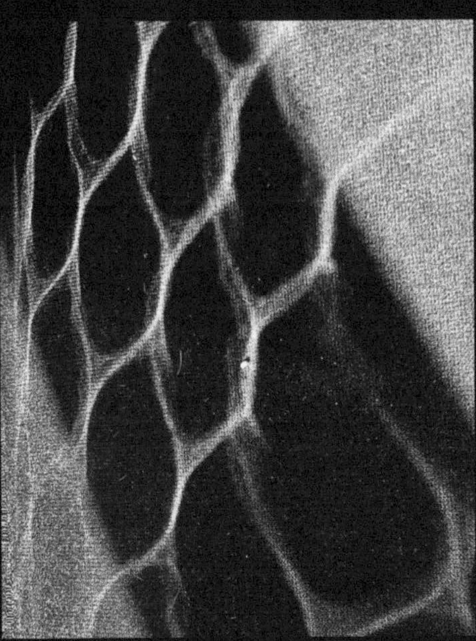

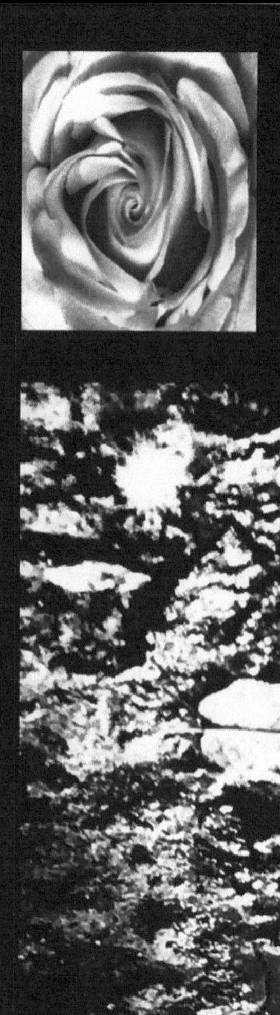

Like dominos fall, one dark day comes;
the another; then tens; even scores.

Life started to prove that saying true,
and I quote, 'when it rains, it pours.'

Life dips its ruler, to measure
our perseverance and aim,

We try to remember a way to stay strong,
so, our goals, we still can claim.

The ones we love, and the
ones we thought loved,
may someday not be found.

Regardless, go out and love again,
'til body marries the ground.

So live your life and yield, no more,
to the things that dull your spark...

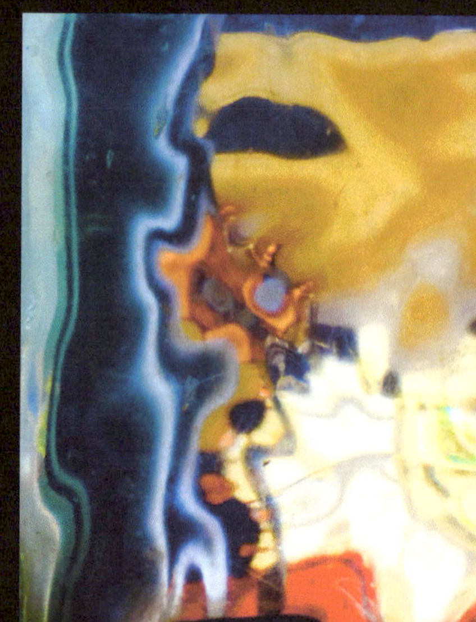

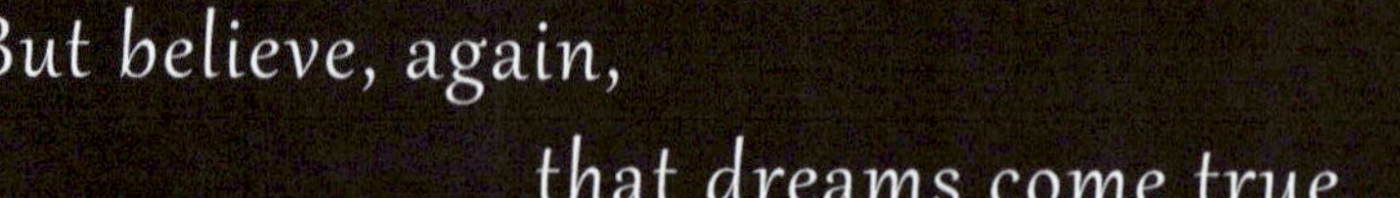

But believe, again,

that dreams come true...

...and we can live Outside the Dark.